STORY OF PRIDE, POWER AND UPLIFT

Annie T. Malone

Story of Pride, Power and Uplift: Annie T. Malone is part of THE GREAT HEARTLANDERS SERIES. This collection of biographies for children describes the lives of local heroes – men and women of all races and careers – who have made lasting contributions to the nation and the world.

STORY OF PRIDE, POWER AND UPLIFT:
Annie T. Malone

Copyright © 2003 by Acorn Books

Acorn Books
7337 Terrace
Kansas City, MO 64114

Cataloging-in-Publication Data
J.L. Wilkerson
    Story of Pride, Power and Uplift: Annie T. Malone / by
J. L. Wilkerson
    Library of Congress Control Number: 2002093845
    Series Title: The Great Heartlanders Series
ISBN 0-9664470-8-5
1. Annie Turnbo Malone, 1869-1957 - Juvenile literature.
2. St. Louis - Missouri - Chicago - Illinois - Biography -
History - Juvenile literature - Cosmetology - Entrepreneur -
Businesswoman - Midwest.

10 9 8 7 6 5 4 3 2 1

Dedication

For all the friends and supporters of THE GREAT HEARTLANDERS SERIES who understand the importance of providing children the opportunity to learn about their local heroes.

Acknowledgements

Thanks to Betty Dixon for her careful attention to detail. Appreciation to Andra Chase for her fine artwork. Gratitude to John Parkison for his help with photographs and to Christopher Migneron for his research assistance.

Book production by Acorn Books, Kansas City, Missouri.

Image Credits:
Library of Congress, pages 19 and 58.
Missouri Historical Society, pages 38, 39 and 41.
Chicago Historical Society, cover and pages 54, 84, 92, 96 and 99.
Rolls Royce Motor Cars Company, page 74.
Annie Malone Children and Family Service Center, page 77.

Contents

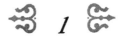

A Celebration, Chicago, August 25, 1950

Annie T. Malone watched the little girl. The child sat lazily in her mother's lap. Her small fingers gently pulled through her mother's hair, twisting and weaving several long strands. The mother chatted with the woman sitting next to her.

The mother and child sat in the middle of an auditorium. Annie could see everyone in the big room because she was in the guest-of-honor seat on the stage. The little girl and her mother were lucky to have a seat. The auditorium was packed. People stood in the aisles.

Throughout the auditorium, the people fanned themselves against Chicago's steamy August heat. Printed in fancy lettering across the cardboard fans were the words: "Annie T. Malone, founder of Poro College, 1900-1950. Fifty Years of Beauty Culture." People in the auditorium had come to celebrate Annie and her work. The 80-year-old businesswoman and her cosmetic business were famous throughout the U.S. and several other countries.

An elbow pressed against Annie's side. Mrs. Lillie Hughes, head of the Chicago office of Annie's company, whispered, "The choir's going to start, Annie."

Fifty black-robed singers lined up below the stage. They swayed to the music from a piano, trumpet and drum.

"Bless her name," the choir sang, "Poro's leader all the way, triumphant for fifty years."

People in the auditorium called, "Amen!"

During the next two hours, other choirs sang. People gave speeches – preachers, judges, business leaders, social workers, politicians. One man said that Annie's success came from faith in herself. Another man said Annie had courage. One woman praised Annie's generosity. The key to Annie's success, said the woman, was a desire to help her people. Another woman said that Annie loved hard work and had overcome many obstacles.

Annie listened to the praise. She wished all of it were true, but it wasn't. She hadn't always had courage or faith in herself. She hadn't always felt generous. Love hard work? No, Annie didn't love hard work. Hard work was necessary, but she didn't love it. She'd always taken her work seriously – too seriously, some people said. In the last fifty years, she'd faced a tornado, a scandal, near-bankruptcy, betrayal. Sure she'd overcome some of those obstacles, but not all. Some obstacles she'd just wrapped up and hauled along with her, the way you do a heavy suitcase on a long, long trip.

Key to her success? Did she have one? Just one?

Once again Annie noticed the little girl. Seemingly unaware of the music and speeches, the girl's fingers combed through her mother's hair. She worked carefully. She gathered all the stray hairs, smoothing them together until the strands were fine, black ropes.

Key to success? Annie suddenly thought she knew the answer. And she'd learned it when she was no bigger than that little girl, back when the long, long trip began.

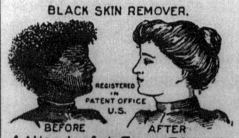
By the time the 20ᵗʰ century began, the line separating the black and white races was clearly drawn. Black people were stereotyped in American culture. In books, newspapers and theater, they were shown with wild hair and apelike facial features. Many manufacturers of shampoos and cosmetics claimed that their products would change the stereotypes. These companies — both black and white — promised to make black people's hair straight and to transform their skin into white, or at least to make it much less dark. Such promises implied that white skin was more attractive than black skin. Unfortunately, skin bleaches were dangerous. Some contained lead-based paint that could cause sickness and death.

Annie T. Malone refused to sell skin bleach and hair straightening products. She fought against the use of these products. She urged African Americans to have pride in their appearance. She developed a beauty system that encouraged black people to dress and act with dignity.

[This advertisement appeared in The Colored American Magazine, 1903.]

2

Death's Door,
Peoria, Illinois, 1875

The kitchen was warm. Annie's sister Sarah kept the fire burning in the black stove night and day. Only along the bottom of the door and the cracks in the windowsill did the cold winter winds find a way inside the little house.

Three years earlier, Annie came to live with her sister. Sarah kept the little girl's cot next to the stove. Annie was sickly. She was often so weak that she stayed in bed for days at a time.

Annie stood on a wooden crate by the wash tub. She was short for a nine-year-old, and she needed the crate to reach her sister's head. Sarah sat perfectly still while Annie parted and plaited long rows of her hair. Annie wore three sweaters and a pair of leggings. Sarah, who constantly worried that her little sister was at "death's door," made her wear the thick trousers for warmth.

Two women sat around the kitchen table watching Annie work on Sarah's hair.

"The girl's got that knack," said Lillie, one of the women. "She can do hair like nobody's business."

"And it's gonna *be* my business," Annie said. She kept working on her sister's hair and didn't look toward the women at the table.

They'd had this conversation many times. It was often a point of heated discussion. Annie insisted that she would someday earn a living by styling women's hair. Sarah called it "Annie's Dream." Lillie, who worked as a field hand at a nearby farm, said Annie better stop having such silly dreams. Black women had to earn a living and job choices were very limited. Farm labor and housekeeping were the jobs available for most black women. Annie had never heard of a black woman earning a living by styling hair.

"You might have the knack," Lillie said to Annie, "but that doesn't mean anything. My granny makes the best fried catfish this side of the Ohio River, but that won't put a roof over her head and clothes on her back."

Sarah said that Annie might get so good at hair-dressing that she could charge a penny or so for the service. "She might earn a little spending money on the side when she gets a real job," Sarah said, encouragingly.

Lillie turned to the second woman at the table. "She'd sure earn a penny if she could fix that hair of yours."

The woman, named Bea, frowned. A blue bandanna covered her head. It hid a large bald spot above her right ear. She looked sadly at Sarah's thick hair. Bea had come by Sarah's house to see if Annie could suggest some way to restore her hair. Six weeks ago Bea bought a hair tonic. It was guaranteed to straighten nappy hair, the traveling salesman said. Bea applied the tonic that very day. The liquid tingled her scalp, like a hundred tiny needles. Four days later her hair began falling out. Within a week, the right side of her head was hairless. And now, a month later, little more than coarse fuzz covered the damaged spot.

Lillie saw Bea's frown. "It's your own fault," Lillie said. "You might as well jump in a river of lye as to put that mess on your hair."

Bea pulled up the edge of the scarf and showed Annie her head. "Can't you do something?" she asked, miserably.

Annie looked at the bald skin. It was blistered and puffy, as if the flesh were burned. She feared that the harsh chemical had forever damaged the hair's roots.

"I thought you'd learned your lesson," Sarah said to Bea.

Last August Bea hurt her hands and arms by using magnolia balm, a skin-bleaching lotion. Like many black women, Bea had tried several dangerous skin-whiteners, such as arsenic tablets and calcimine powders and lotions. Some of the cosmetics sold at that time contained lead-based paint. This caused sickness, sometimes even death, for some users.

A slender woman, Bea had smooth, dark brown skin, the color of a buckeye. Except for today, Bea's big, dark eyes usually sparkled with cheerfulness. She sang in the church choir. The preacher said her musical solos in the church choir sounded like an angel praying. Annie wondered why Bea was always trying to change herself by using bleaches and straighteners.

"Maybe your hair will be better when it grows out," Annie said to Bea.

"*If* it grows out," Lillie said. "More likely a porcupine, that's what it'll look like."

Tears welled up in Bea's eyes. She held her forehead in one hand and shook her head. "All I wanted," she said, choking back a sob, "was to look nice…you know, be pretty."

❧ 3 ❧

The Old Woman in the Woods

A few days later, Annie woke in the middle of the night. She could barely breathe. She pulled at the neck of her nightgown and gasped for air. Sarah, hearing the commotion, ran into the kitchen. She quickly set a pot of water on the stove and started a fire. From a clay jar, she grabbed a handful of crushed leaves and tossed them into the pot.

Less than a minute later, she bundled up Annie and opened the back door. A blast of winter wind blew around them. When its sudden chill swept across Annie's face, the girl gasped, taking in a lung full of air.

Seeing that her sister could breathe, though with difficulty, Sarah closed the door. She carried Annie to the stove where the water simmered. A sharp,

11

rich smell rose up from the pot with the leaves, and Sarah held Annie's face over the steam.

The pot was nearly boiled dry when Sarah finally laid Annie back on the cot. By then the girl's breathing was almost normal, but she was so exhausted that she fell asleep before Sarah had smoothed out the last blanket.

Annie stayed in bed for three days. When she was better, she asked to go to school, but Sarah said no. Annie was at "death's door," Sarah said.

Finally one sunny day in April, when the temperature rose into the 70s, Sarah let Annie go outside. Sarah wanted the girl to go on an errand. She was to buy herbs from the woman who lived in the woods east of town. Sarah handed the clay jar to Annie. "Don't dawdle," Sarah warned. "And come straight back."

———

The path to the woman's cabin ran off the highway, across an open field, and wound through a thick grove of walnut trees. Near the creek, the trail suddenly twisted up and over a steep hill. The cabin stood beside a little pond whose waters trickled into the creek during the spring.

The woman worked in her front yard garden. Wearing a large apron with a dozen pockets, the woman gathered leaves and flower buds and put them in the pockets. She was an herbalist.

When Annie handed her the clay pot, the woman said, "You still having those spells, Annie Turnbo?"

Annie nodded and the woman said, as she always did – for the two of them talked about this every time Annie came for herbs – "You'll grow out of those spells. Mark my word."

Annie followed the woman into the little cabin. The smell of flowers and herbs filled the front room. Cut and tied in bunches, plants hung from the ceiling. Shelves with rows of glass jars lined the walls. Some jars were filled with colorful dried herbs. Some jars held herbs floating in liquids.

The woman put three jars on her worktable. From each of the jars, she shook herbs into a stone bowl. As she stirred and crushed the leaves with a short wooden mallet, Annie wandered around the room. She read the labels on the glass jars. "*Rosemary,*" said one label. Below the herb's name were the words, "Heals the joints. Prevents nightmares."

Other herbs included: "*Foxglove*. Mends the heart." "*Snakeroot*. Heals moon madness." "*Drooping willow*. Soothes the headache." "*Valerian root*. Brings sleep." "*Red Cardinal*. Cures the cramps and fever." "*Tansy*. Prevents decay." "*Rose Petals*. Eye tonic." "*Rue*. Removes insects." "*Sage*. Cures coughs." "*Feverfew*. Cures rheumatism."

"Do you have anything for hair?" Annie asked. "A plant that grows hair."

The woman poured the crushed leaves into Annie's clay jar. She then pulled several glass jars from the shelves. "No," the woman said. "I have many." She took samples from each jar and mixed them in the stone bowl. She shook the mixture into a bottle and then poured a creamy yellow liquid from one of the bottles. She called it her Hair Elixir. "Just rub it into your scalp and let it sit for 30 minutes and wash it out." She handed the bottle and clay jar to Annie. "That'll be one dime."

When Annie carried the Hair Elixir home that day, she had wanted to help Bea recover from the bad hair tonic. She had no way of knowing that the ingredients in that little bottle – and other ingredients that Annie would eventually add – would change her life.

4

A Human Experiment

Annie tried the hair-growing herbs on Bea's scalp. At first Bea was pleased. Several days after Annie applied the herbs, the bald spot sprouted hair, long and thick. In the end, however, the results were disappointing. The new hair was as dry and lifeless as straw. Bea's disappointment saddened Annie.

If only there was some way to restore the hair's softness, as well as help it to grow. During the next several months, Annie visited the old woman in the woods. But none of the woman's herbs and potions helped with the dry, lifeless hair.

Although Annie was often too sick to go to school, she studied her lessons at home.

She was very interested in her science lessons, especially chemistry. Maybe she could discover some chemical that helped grow, as well as soften, hair. The school for black children, which Annie attended, didn't have chemistry books. Bea's mother, however, cleaned the white children's school each Saturday, and the white teacher gave Bea's mother permission to borrow one of the chemistry textbooks. Annie studied the book during the next week.

At the corner grocery, Annie bought all sorts of ointments and lotions. She mixed together various combinations of them. She also added some of the old woman's herbs to the store-bought liquids.

One day Sarah found Annie holding a kitten she'd found in the alley. The cat suffered from mange, a disease causing hair loss. Annie rubbed something onto the hairless back. Sarah picked up the jar.

"What are you doing with bag balm?" Sarah asked, and then added with a laugh, "Annie Minerva Turnbo, you planning on being a farmer?"

Annie knew farmers used balm to soften chapped cow udders. But she wanted to test its effect on bald skin. She had already dabbed the cat's bald skin with the lotions and herbs she had mixed together.

16

Sarah said she worried about Annie. She didn't worry about her sister being sickly. In fact, Annie was growing stronger every year. Sarah worried that Annie never seemed to rest from studying chemistry and herbs. "I don't think you know how to have fun," Sarah said.

"This *is* fun," Annie said. She said it so seriously that Sarah wondered if Annie even knew what the word "fun" meant. As if reading her sister's mind, Annie added, "I'm looking for a way to fix Bea's hair – and other women's damaged hair. It's fun."

One spring day Annie watched Sarah sprinkle seeds in a large, soil-filled box next to the house. Sarah then covered the box with a piece of glass. The soil inside the covered box, called a cold frame, was warmed under the spring sun. The warmth helped germinate the seeds. Within a few days the seeds sprouted. Every day Annie went outside to watch their progress. Even on cold days, the heat under the glass-covered cold frame helped the tender plants to grow. Each day they seemed one or two inches taller.

Maybe heat would help grow healthy hair. Annie tested her theory on another friend of Sarah. The woman had applied hydrogen peroxide to her hair and left the harsh bleach on for so long that it burned away half her hair. Her scalp looked as if it had caught fire.

Annie first treated the red, blistered scalp with a thick cream, made of lotions and herbs. She then wrapped the woman's head in moist, warm towels. At first the woman's eyes filled with tears. The touch of the heated towels on her burned scalp was painful.

Every five minutes Annie replaced the towels with fresh warm ones. Within fifteen minutes the woman was smiling. The pain was gone.

Forty-five minutes later, Annie removed the towels and gently washed away all the cream. The skin was pink from the heat, but it looked healthy. Even the blisters seemed to have disappeared.

With a clean cloth, Annie applied a dark lotion to the woman's scalp. She explained that this would help heal the hair follicles – the glands under the skin.

"I just want my hair back," said the woman.

Annie gave her a jar of the herbal mixture. She told the woman to apply the mixture twice a day. When the woman asked how long it would take, Annie said she didn't know. "You're my first human experiment," she said.

The woman's hand shot up to her head in alarm. She obviously didn't like the idea of being an "experiment."

Six weeks later the woman returned. Hair was growing all over her head. It was short but healthy. She put 25 cents on Sarah's kitchen counter. She said she wanted to buy another jar of the "herb physic."

For the next ten years, Annie continued perfecting her hair shampoos and treatments. Word about the success of her lotions spread throughout the

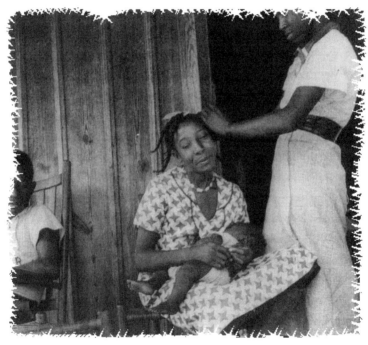

Years later, when Annie started her hair-care company, one of her women employees said that every black neighborhood had an "official hair wrapper." She said that women came together because it was "fun working on each other's heads."

When Annie decided to sell her products throughout the country, she tapped into this ready-made market of women who enjoyed working on others' hair.

neighborhood. Black women in Peoria eagerly bought her "Wonderful Hair Grower," the name that Annie gave to the mixture. Soon Annie and Sarah had to buy bigger pots and bowls to mix the ingredients for the increasing number of customers.

Annie sold her hair-care mixtures as a way to make extra money. No one knows how she earned her living during those years in Peoria. What is certain, however, is that Annie still dreamed of turning her hair-care sales into a full-time business. But in order to do that, she would need to find more customers than just the women in Peoria.

In 1899, Annie told Sarah that she wanted to move to Lovejoy, Illinois. Lovejoy was a town founded by African Americans. There were hundreds more black women in Lovejoy than lived in Peoria – hundreds more who would learn about the Wonderful Hair Grower.

5

The Ideal American Beauty, Lovejoy, Illinois, 1900

In Lovejoy, Annie rented a back room in a small, wooden building. For the rest of her life Annie remembered that building. In the years to come, her company became an enormous success, and she would construct one of the largest buildings in St. Louis, Missouri – but all of that would be more than 15 years in the future. Annie always remembered it all started in a little room in Lovejoy, Illinois, at the beginning of a new century.

The rent for the office space was $5.00 a month. Annie wrote the amount on a piece of paper. Under it, she listed other dollar figures. One represented how much she figured she and Sarah would spend on food for a month. Other amounts represented how much they would need for transportation, donations to church, household supplies and ingredients for the Wonderful Hair Grower. She added up the list of numbers and showed the total to Sarah.

21

Annie said, "That's how much we have to earn this month – *if* we hope to be here a second month."

Next Annie walked around the little town. She strolled up every street and down every alley. She took notes, recording the location of the church and drug store. She and Sarah arrived on Monday, wash day, and Annie noticed which clotheslines held women's clothes. She estimated the number of women who lived in Lovejoy. They were all potential Wonderful Hair Grower customers. When she returned to the small rented office, Annie drew a map of the town. She divided the map into six sections.

The next day, just as the sun rose above the eastern horizon, Annie set out down the streets of Lovejoy. She held the map with the six sections. Annie went door to door each day for five days. On the sixth day, she went to church in the morning. In the afternoon she visited houses on the map's sixth section. By the end of the week, Annie had met every woman in Lovejoy.

Most women in town already used some type of hair care product. Most of the time these products were nothing more than jars of goose fat or other heavy oil. Some women of Lovejoy doubted Annie's claims about the Wonderful Hair Grower. Annie later recalled, "I went around in the buggy and made speeches, demonstrated the shampoo on myself, and talked about cleanliness and hygiene, until they realized I was right."

One day, a girl, probably no older than 15 years, came to Annie's office. The girl's long wavy hair was pulled back and fastened at the back of her neck. She had covered the top of her head with a big scarf, as if she were trying to hide her hair. Despite the girl's efforts, the tight curls and waves poked out from the edges of the bun and scarf. The young girl laid a newspaper on Annie's worktable. She then opened it to the second page and pointed to a drawing of a young girl.

"Will you make my hair look like this?" the girl asked, almost pleading.

The drawing was part of an advertisement. Large letters under the drawing said, "The Gibson Girl – the Ideal American Beauty." The pictured woman was white and had smooth, lush hair.

Annie studied the picture. How

The Gibson Girl

could the girl in the newspaper be the ideal of beauty? Most women didn't look like the white Gibson Girl.

"I've tried everything to straighten my hair," said the girl. "Fat. Soap. Nothing works." She pulled the scarf from her hair. Her black curls sprang about her head like a storm cloud. "See what I mean?"

Annie later learned that women all over the country were trying to model themselves after the Gibson Girl. They saw newspapers and magazines showing the "Gibson Girl," said by advertisers to be the ideal American beauty. Some women attached weights to their hair in order to pull out the curls. Some women flattened their hair with heated irons. Like black women, Jewish women rubbed heavy oils in their hair to soften tight waves. Annie knew that black women often tried to straighten their hair by smearing on goose fat and laundry soap.

This saddened Annie. Why would women want to pattern themselves after such a narrow idea of beauty?

Annie led the girl to a chair. "You're too beautiful to try to look like someone you're not." Annie tied a large apron around the girl's neck. The girl's eyes lit up when Annie said that she would give her hair the Wonderful Hair Grower treatment.

"Just like the Gibson Girl?" asked the girl.

Annie stood in front of the teenager, whose name was Alice. "No. I can't do that...and wouldn't try, even if I could. But I won't do anything until you stop talking about the Gibson Girl. Agreed?"

After a moment, Alice nodded. "But I'm tired of it in my eyes." Alice said she was enrolled in stenographer's school, but her hair kept falling in her eyes when she tried to take dictation. In the summer, the long, thick strands caused the sweat to roll down her neck and back.

Annie washed and combed Alice's hair. She told the girl that the hair care mixtures weren't meant to make black women look like the Gibson Girl. Annie's shampoos and lotions cleaned off the fat and heavy oils and left the hair soft and manageable. As she talked, Annie trimmed Alice's hair, then rolled the edges into a tight roll in the back. The neck was clear of hair. Annie gathered wisps of hair hanging loosely around the girl's face and fastened them neatly under two fancy combs.

Alice stared at her finished hairstyle in a large round mirror. It was clean and neat, and it framed her face in a flattering way. And what's more, the wisps of hair were off her neck and out of her eyes.

Annie removed the apron and swept the hair clippings outside in the alley. She picked up Alice's scarf and tied it around the girl's neck.

"I'd say you look like an ideal American beauty," she said.

Annie asked Alice if she would like a job selling the Wonderful Hair Grower. The popularity of Annie's hair products had grown so much that she and Sarah couldn't keep up with the demand in Peoria and Lovejoy. Alice was so enthusiastic about the job offer that she started to work that afternoon.

Within a year of arriving in Lovejoy, Annie hired two other women to help with the growing business. The saleswomen went door to door showing and selling Annie's shampoo and hair grower.

Early in 1902, Alice came into Annie's office and laid a newspaper on her boss's desk. Annie didn't even look at the page. She frowned at Alice. "Is this another 'Ideal American Beauty'?" Annie asked.

Alice laughed and waved the paper in front of Annie. "Here's your chance," Alice said.

Annie looked at the paper. Huge letters announced

THE LOUISIANA PURCHASE EXPOSITION.
Meet the world in St. Louis in 1903.
People from around the country,
Representatives from every corner of the world
Will be in St. Louis, Missouri, in 1903
At
The World's Fair.

Annie had become the first black woman to start a hair care company for black women. In the years to come she would celebrate 1900 as the year that she started her business in Lovejoy, Illinois. But Annie had dreams of offering her hair products to black women far beyond Lovejoy.

Alice was right. The World's Fair was Annie's big chance to expand the company's market throughout the United States – and throughout the world. Thousands of people would visit St. Louis during the fair. Annie and her Wonderful Hair Grower would be there.

Annie's parents, Robert and Isabella Turnbo, were slaves in Kentucky. During the Civil War, her father fought on the Union side. After the war, the Turnbo family moved to Metropolis, Illinois, on the banks of the Ohio River. Before Annie was school age, Robert and Isabella died, and Annie was sent to live with a married sister in Peoria.

After developing several beauty-care products, Annie moved to Lovejoy, named for Elijah Lovejoy, an abolitionist. The town is now called Brooklyn.

Annie's company eventually found international success after she moved to St. Louis. Before the Civil War, that city was the biggest slave market in Missouri. By the time Annie moved to the river town, most black people (67%) in Missouri lived in big cities like St. Louis, Kansas City and Springfield. This percentage was three times the national average.

National segregation laws helped push blacks into separate neighborhoods. Some of these neighborhoods were overcrowded. Often places of poverty, filth and crime, they acquired names like Hog Alley (Jefferson City), The Bowery (Kansas City) and Clabber Alley (St. Louis). Living in separate neighborhoods, however, did not protect African Americans from bigotry. Between 1889 and 1918 mobs in Missouri lynched 51 black people, more than in some southern states, such as Virginia and North Carolina.

6

The World's Fair, 1904, St. Louis, Missouri

The noise. That was the first thing Annie noticed about St. Louis. The big city never seemed to sleep. In the mornings, milk wagons clattered down the streets. Ice wagons rattled in the afternoons. Fire engines clanged at all times, day and night. A cart, buggy or wagon was always racing by. Annie felt that she took her life in her hands when she stepped off the curb.

Annie rented a four-room flat near downtown St. Louis. Sarah stayed behind in Illinois because she didn't like the idea of living in the big city. Annie also wondered if she'd made a mistake leaving peaceful Lovejoy. The noise of St. Louis kept Annie awake at first, but within a few days she slept soundly all night.

Shortly after moving to St. Louis, Annie gathered her sample case and started knocking on doors around the neighborhood. While in Lovejoy, Annie

re-searched and experimented with a variety of skin-care products. By now she had added cleansing cream, moisturizer, face powder and other cosmetics to her line of products. A woman's appearance depended on healthy skin just as much as on healthy hair.

The Market Street area where Annie lived was an African American community. Single-family homes and apartments lined nearby streets. Grocers, butchers, fabric stores, millinery shops, drug stores, churches, a bank and a newspaper office were all within walking distance. For the most part, the black and white races lived separately in the city. But Annie had no intention of staying only within her neighborhood.

Annie looked forward to the World's Fair. Called the Louisiana Purchase Exposition, the fair was in honor of Pres. Thomas Jefferson's signing of the 1803 Louisiana Purchase. Scheduled to open in 1903, construction on the fairgrounds progressed more slowly than planned. The new opening date was changed to April 1904.

Annie learned that more than 10,000 laborers worked on building the exposition. Many of them camped in Forest Park, where huge buildings and waterways for the fair were being constructed. Annie discovered all this from a woman named Ruby Warren, a laundress who lived nearby. Ruby's sister lived in the park with her husband. The couple had moved from Mississippi to work at the fairgrounds. Macie, the sister, cooked for a large crew of men, and her husband hauled trash from the construction site.

One day Annie asked a peddler with a little donkey cart to give her a ride to the west end of Forest Park. The peddler sold supplies to workers living on the fairgrounds. It was early February 1904, just two months before the fair's opening.

Annie was astonished when she saw the exposition buildings. The west side of the park, once called The Wilderness, was now almost treeless. Now a dozen, enormous buildings, like Greek and Roman temples, stood out in white starkness against the barren park.

Hundreds of workers lived around the edges of the fairgrounds. They lived in old streetcars and tents. Macie and her husband lived in a shed made of leftover construction material.

When Annie introduced herself, Macie looked at her curiously, even suspiciously. Annie's hair was perfectly cut and combed. Her tailored black coat was clean, and her polished shoes were stylish. The little carpetbag she carried looked as if she'd just arrived on a first-class railcar. Macie wore a food-splattered apron. An old shawl draped her head and shoulders.

Macie went back to stirring stew in a large kettle. In a thick southern accent, she asked, "Now why would a fancy lady like you come all the way out here to stand in the mud with Macie Allen?"

Annie nodded, as if she approved of Macie's wary attitude. "You're from the south, from Mississippi. And I'm wanting some names of people living in the south. Your sister says you're looking for work, something more than being a cook. I believe we can help each other."

Macie stared at Annie. What could she possibly do for this handsome looking black woman? What could the woman do for her? And then a thought suddenly dawned on Macie. Once again she was annoyed.

"I'm not working as some maid," she said, "or some washerwoman. I've told Ruby, and I'm telling you."

Annie said she wasn't looking for a maid or washerwoman. "I'm hiring saleswomen," she said.

Macie's face brightened for a moment but then quickly darkened. "Selling what?" she asked.

Annie smiled. She liked Macie's spunk. Annie explained about her company. She described the Wonderful Hair Grower and the other products. Annie said she wanted to hire Macie and several other women to sell the products.

With a laugh, Macie pulled off her ragged shawl, revealing a mat of tangled hair. She said she didn't think she'd make a very good hair-care saleswoman.

"We're going to fix that right now," Annie said. She picked up the carpetbag. In a little while, she talked Macie into letting Annie shampoo and style her hair. Inside the shed, Annie pulled all her supplies from the bag and started heating water over a small stove. Within two hours, Annie washed, combed and styled Macie's hair.

Macie sat in front of the hand-held mirror. The transformation was amazing. The hand mirror didn't show her shapeless dress, a hand-me-down from her sister. It didn't show the apron, splattered with gravy and smeared with soot. It only showed a lovely face and head. She might have passed as a salesclerk or secretary in one of the offices near Annie's building.

Macie agreed to work for Annie. Annie had already talked Ruby into selling the Wonderful Hair Grower door to door. Both women had left the south and come to St. Louis looking for work. After living in St. Louis for almost a year, Ruby struggled to make ends meet as a laundress. Macie and her husband had fled the south after a lynching took place in a town near their home. They never wanted to return to Mississippi.

During the next few weeks, Annie introduced Macie to the company, taught her how to dress properly and how to talk with people about the hair and skin products. Macie went on sales calls with Annie and then she made calls on her own. Before long she was earning a good commission on each sale – earning far more than she'd ever made as a camp cook. Ruby, too, was making a comfortable living selling the beauty-care products.

———

More than 200,000 people turned out for the grand opening of the Louisiana Purchase Exposition on April 30, 1904. The fairgoers listened to speeches and heard John Philip Sousa and his band. Visitors heard concerts on the world's largest pipe organ. The mile-long midway, called The Pike, offered every kind of entertainment and amusement: exotic animals, human contortionists, reenactments of famous battles, launchings of miniature battleships, and displays of historical objects – such as a fire engine once pumped by Pres. George Washington. For 10 cents, visitors rode a little train across the fairgrounds.

Macie introduced Annie to people from all over the United States who had come to participate in the fair. Annie even met natives from the Philippines and members of the Pygmy tribe in Africa. In early August, Annie visited the fair and saw special events featuring people of color from around the world. Later

During the late 19th century, St. Louis often could not supply its residents with clean drinking water. Realizing that people from all over the world would attend the 1904 World's Fair [shown here], the city was forced to make an improvement. One of the advantages of the fair was that the city developed one of the best water purification systems in the country.

that month, she went to a track and field event of the 1904 Olympics. The modern games had started in 1896. The 1904 World's Fair was the first time in history that the United States hosted the games. Annie watched George Coleman Poage, the only

African American in the Olympics. From Milwaukee, Wisconsin, he was the first black person to win a medal in the modern games.

During the evenings, approximately 15,000 people stayed overnight at the Louisiana Exposition. [Festival Hall is shown here.] The Inside Inn was a hotel on the fairgrounds. It was run by a staff of 1,000 and could accommodate 4,000 guests. Other people who lived at the fair included the Jefferson Guard police force, firefighters, and state and foreign commissioners and their staffs. Several thousand military personnel camped on the fairgrounds.

One night after a concert, Annie and Macie sat outside of Festival Hall [shown on page 39]. They watched thousands of electric lights shine on the great, round building. The lights changed colors from time to time. They sparkled in the cascading fountains that ran along the wide, front stairways.

The spectacle of the fair thrilled Annie. She didn't even mind the bustle and noise. In fact, she was beginning to love the noise of St. Louis. It made her feel a part of the highly energetic city.

The theme of the fair was "Life and Motion." That would be Annie's theme, too, she decided.

Life and motion. For Annie, life was the work that lay ahead – the possibilities of her company and what it could mean for people like Alice and Ruby and Macie.

New products, new salespeople, new places – Annie's company was in motion. She dreamed of expanding it far beyond St. Louis. New places! Her dream extended to every state in the Union…and she planned to begin in the south.

Construction of the Fair Grounds began on September 3, 1901. The fair was supposed to open in 1903 but was delayed until April 30, 1904. The fair ended on December 1, 1904. The average daily attendance during the last three months of the fair was 92,000 people. The record attendance was on September 15 – called St. Louis Day – when

358,405 came to the fair. During the entire seven months, 12,800,000 people bought tickets to the fair. A ticket cost 50 cents. Considering the number of free admissions, organizers believed that the attendance was closer to 20 million. Fair goers had the opportunity to see native people from all over the world, as shown in this photograph.

7

In the South,
Mississippi, 1905

Macie was proud that she could read and write. Not many black children learned those skills in Mississippi where Macie grew up. She drew a map of her hometown and wrote the names of several landmarks near the section of town where the black people lived.

Annie planned to visit Mississippi. If she wanted to sell her products throughout the U.S.A., why not start in the south where most black people lived?

Annie traveled by train. Besides the sample case holding her cosmetic products, she packed a bag with sandwiches and a thermos of coffee. During the trip, Annie kept busy. She read the *St. Louis Paladium,* a newspaper written by and about black people. Annie also made notes to herself in a little notebook. She wrote long columns of numbers. She calculated how much she spent (her expenses)

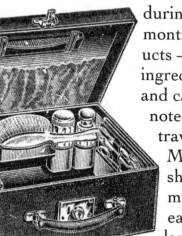

during the last six months on her products – herbs and other ingredients, bottles and caps. She also noted office rent and travel expenses to Mississippi. Then she calculated how much she had earned during the last six months.

Five saleswomen worked for Annie now. Each woman earned a percentage of every sale that she made. The rest of the money was turned over to Annie.

Annie added up both columns. She totaled the expenses column and then the earnings column. She then subtracted the expenses from the earnings. Ever since Annie started the business five years earlier, she had made a profit (the difference between earnings and expenses). The profit now was greater than it had ever been. And what's more, five women – her sales crew – were making their livings doing clean, honest work.

As the train neared Macie's hometown, the black man seated next to Annie warned her against getting off at the town's depot. Emotions still ran hot about the lynching that happened a few months earlier. Annie knew about the murder. That was the

44

reason Macie and her husband fled to St. Louis. Annie thanked the man for his concern. Though she had misgivings, Annie told him she had work to do in the town. Annie gathered her products sample case and small travel bag and headed toward the train door. She was the only person traveling in the black people's car who disembarked at the town.

When she stepped from the train and looked down the main street, Annie didn't see any black people. It was Saturday morning. Shoppers bustled from the barbershop, the hotel, restaurant, grocery and feed store. All white.

Macie had told Annie to go to the black church. She had drawn and labeled it on the map. The church was south of the depot at the far end of town, just past the reservoir. Annie picked up her bags and started down Main Street. Every head turned to watch the elegantly dressed black woman stride down the dirt road, gliding along so smoothly that she hardly stirred the fine red dust.

Annie stared off down the street. She focused far into the distance, at that point where the street's edges seemed to meet, like an arrow pointing her beyond those staring eyes. Just as Annie passed the barbershop, a group of men began to shout at her. A few more people joined in, calling out insults as she continued walking. Annie ignored the ugly words. She tried to forget about the lynching. She was tempted to quicken her pace, to move as swiftly as possible past the business district. She resisted the temptation, however. To run – to flee – seemed so cowardly, so undignified.

Suddenly a tall man who stood near the general store threw something. It was a rock, and it hit the fullness of her black skirt, made a dull thudding sound and rolled harmlessly to the ground. Annie didn't bat an eye. She walked, straight toward that arrow's tip, toward her destination.

Soon Annie was past the town limits. A few minutes later, she stood at a crossroad marked by a tall catalpa tree, which was clearly drawn on Macie's map. Annie turned and headed east. She began to feel herself relax. And yet for the first time, she noticed that her heart was pounding and sweat ran down her arms and back. She passed several houses. Black women sat on the porches stringing beans and husking corn. Black men in wide-brimmed hats hoed weeds in kitchen gardens.

Forty minutes after leaving the train, Annie stood beside the water pump on the church lawn. She drank a cup of the cool water. The rock had left a thin dusty trail down her skirt. She brushed off the dust.

A large, elderly woman in a calico dress stepped from a back door of the church. She wiped her hands on an apron and studied the stranger by the water pump. Annie introduced herself, said she was a friend of Macie and Ruby. Immediately the woman's eyes brightened. She asked how "those babies" were. Before long Annie and the woman were working together in the church kitchen. Annie helped prepare the supper for the church's Saturday fish fry.

That night Annie talked to more than 20 church women about her cosmetics and hair-products. Annie offered to come to each of their homes and demonstrate the products.

The women asked why they had to meet separately. Why couldn't they all meet together? Wouldn't that be more fun? Annie wondered how she could possibly teach about her products and her business in a crowd of women who were having "fun." And then she remembered her sister, Sarah, who said that Annie had a hard time having "fun."

Annie agreed to have a group meeting. With permission from the preacher, the women met in the church. Just a lot of women playing with their hair, he had said. What harm could there be in that?

And of course there wasn't any harm. Not in a direct way. Nevertheless, of the 25 women who came to the meeting, 11 became saleswomen for Annie. Some people didn't like that. These eleven women – four single, two widowed, five married and one of those with eight children – now had the means to earn a living. Most people, including the fathers and husbands of the saleswomen, liked the extra income. In many cases, a woman's salary from selling hair and cosmetic products was greater than a farmhand could earn working in the cotton fields. Some people believed, however, that the men were heads of their households, and therefore needed to earn more money than the women. As Annie's business grew and spread throughout the country, this situation became a troubling issue in some places.

On the evening after her first meeting with the 25 Mississippi women, Annie happened to look down at the *Palladium*, the newspaper she brought from St. Louis. In an editorial, the newspaper's editor, John Wheeler, encouraged black people to work hard. He said they should not depend on other people – not on white people, not on politicians, not even on their neighbors – to advance in the world. To succeed, each person needed to make his or her own way in the world. Be self-reliant, as Wheeler had said.

Annie agreed. The Mississippi experience changed Annie's entire business plan. Once upon a time, she imagined expanding her business by teaching one woman at a time. But now she realized the benefits of approaching her business as if it were a school. A school with many classrooms would allow the business to expand rapidly. Annie could teach about her products and methods of selling in a class full of potential saleswomen – black women eager to be self-reliant.

8

A Public Announcement

The day after Annie arrived home to St. Louis from Mississippi, she contacted every black newspaper in the city. She even sent telegrams to major black publications in other cities. She announced a press conference.

Pride, Power and Uplift.
Annie Turnbo announces
the launching of the world's first company
created by and for Negro Women –
Poro Company.

Annie invited the reporters to her office on Market Street at noon the next Friday.

Annie's sales crew – now including seven women – was stunned by the news. What was "Poro"? Macie, Ruby and Alice, who had moved from Lovejoy, were sure no reporters would show up on the day of the conference. Why would the *Paladium*, one of the most important black newspapers in the midwest, send a reporter to such a small, unknown business, especially one run by a woman?

That Friday morning, Macie paced back and forth at the front window. Her heart skipped a beat when anyone walked past the building or even slowed down on the sidewalk. Alice thought some reporters might telephone, and she sat by the phone, which Annie recently had installed. Alice was the only saleswoman confident enough to use the new device. Ruby kept running into Annie's office. She was determined to bolster her boss's hurt feelings when no reporters showed up. The other four saleswomen huddled together in the main room, whispering nervously.

Finally Annie stepped to her office door. For a moment she watched her worried employees. Then she assigned each woman a job...make enough coffee for everyone, including the expected reporters...line up the chairs so reporters could have a place to sit...display samples of the products on a table. Annie told Alice to go to a nearby bakery for a pound cake to offer the reporters. Before returning to her office again, she sent Ruby next door to the stenographer's office. Annie wanted a typed paper with a description of every product, and she wanted enough copies for all the reporters.

At ten minutes until noon, Macie stepped outside on the sidewalk. She looked up and down the busy street. Horse carts and automobiles drove by. Pedestrians walked by. Not a reporter was in sight.

Fifteen minutes later a tall, slender man came into the building. He wore a wrinkled suit and tie and Panama hat. Annie came from her office and greeted him, offered to take his hat and directed him to a chair. He was no sooner seated than three more reporters came into the room.

At twelve thirty every chair was taken. Annie stood before the seated reporters. The room became quiet. Although she was short, Annie held her back so straight and her shoulders so square that she looked much taller. Her voice was even, and she spoke clearly. She didn't speak loudly, however. In fact, her voice was almost too soft for public speaking. Because she looked so impressive, so serious, the reporters made an extra effort to listen to each word.

Annie faced the men confidently. She wasn't confident about speaking in front of strangers, but she was confident about her company. Annie knew exactly where the company was going – and why it was going there. Annie's company would change the black community. It would change the lives of her people.

To help women style their hair, Annie invented a special comb, which she patented in 1900. It was made of steel with widely spaced teeth, designed especially for black women. The comb could be heated on a stove. Some historians believe it was the first modern hot comb.

Knowing that Annie often appeared overly serious, Macie had urged her to smile when talking to the reporters. "Don't look like you're going to bite their heads off," she warned her boss. But Annie forgot. Not even the slightest hint of a smile crossed her face when she finally spoke. Annie told the reporters that her company was now called "Poro." She explained that Poro was a West African word meaning physical and spiritual growth. "That's the company's name," she said, "and that's its purpose."

One of the reporters snickered and called out, "Be serious, Miss Turnbo. You're just selling hair soap and face paints. It's not like you're another Dr. Carver."

The reporter was talking about George Washington Carver, the famous black scientist and teacher. His work to improve the soil had helped farmers all over the world.

For the first time Annie smiled. It was as if the reporter had touched on the very idea she had hoped to get across. "That is exactly what Poro will do – improve the soil...the soil on which our women can build their lives," she said grandly.

The reporters shook their heads in disbelief. They had come here for information, not for some heavy-handed public relations speech. Two of the men closed their notebooks as if they were preparing to leave. One reporter called out mockingly, "How's a woman going to build a life on skin bleach and hair straightener?"

"No, you don't understand," Annie said. She was new at public speaking, and she hadn't expected such negative reactions. Annie's vision was clear to her. She didn't realize it would be so hard to make other people see it.

When two reporters stood up to leave, she raised a hand, as if pleading with them to stay. "Listen. Don't you see? A woman can't succeed – no one can – unless she feels good about herself." She held up an editorial by *Palladium*'s John Wheeler in which the editor had said that black people had to have pride in themselves before they could hope to have power. Annie pointed out that slavery had ended forty years earlier, and yet most black people still lived like slaves.

"How are you to feel good about yourself when the only work you can ever hope for is some dead-end job as a field hand or laundress or some other low-paying job? How can you have pride in your-self when after such backbreaking work you come home looking like someone who's slaved in the cotton fields all day?"

One of the reporters said that a little face powder wasn't going to change the facts of post-slavery America.

"Jobs," she replied quickly. "Poro Company will give women meaningful work. They'll make a decent living." Annie said that at her company hardworking women could advance and achieve a bright future. Annie turned to the man who had talked about skin bleach and hair straighteners. "Poro gives women the resources for enhancing their appearance, not destroying their bodies. We don't sell bleaches and straighteners." Annie then introduced Macie, Ruby and Alice. She told about their former jobs. "Poro products helped them discover their own special beauty."

When some of the reporters still looked unconvinced, Annie said, "Don't under estimate the importance of the way a person looks – a person's appearance. This is more than vanity. A good appearance helps build pride. A good job helps build power. Pride and power, that's Poro's formula for success."

One of the reporters said, "That's a pretty big promise. So, you're saying that this new company of yours – Poro – is going to change the lives of black women in St. Louis."

"No," said Annie. "I'm saying that Poro will *be* a community of black women – and not just in St. Louis but *everywhere*."

Annie Malone's beauty system was more than just lotions and shampoos. The world of Poro created a connection with the day-to-day lives of black women. The company was especially important to poor women, like the one in this photograph. Through Annie's leadership, the company provided jobs for women. It promoted the idea of pride in appearance. In addition, it pledged a large portion of its profits to the black community.

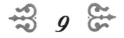

9

Aaron Malone Arrives

The summer heat hung in the air, heavy as a wet towel. Not a leaf on any tree moved. Annie sat at a picnic table. She fanned herself with a handkerchief.

This was the nineteenth church rally she had attended in June. Before that, in April and May, she visited a dozen professional conventions. She also traveled to Poro agencies around the country, including places like Denver, Chicago, Philadelphia, New York, San Francisco, Charleston and Ames, Iowa. In between those big cities, she stopped at more little towns than she could remember and spoke at more club meetings than she could count. She had traveled to every state in the union, except Maine and the Dakotas.

Was she tired? Yes, but she couldn't stop.

Annie was now a well-known businesswoman. Just as she had announced to the reporters, she had established the Poro Company. Annie also started a system of beauty salons in most states. The salons sold Poro products and used the Poro beauty-care method taught at the Poro College in St. Louis. Black women, who hoped to operate Poro salons, applied to Annie for that right – called the right to franchise. Eventually thousands of women operated thousands of Poro salons across the country and in several foreign countries.

The Poro company was growing faster than Annie could keep up with it. Macie had said that Annie was too serious *and* too single-minded. "You get yourself pointed in a direction and nothing can turn you around." Macie didn't say this as if it were a virtue. She worried that Annie worked too hard. Macie added darkly, "One of these days you could head straight into quicksand."

Today's speech was over. Annie had told the audience that the women who worked for her company were "evangels of Poro." Poro saleswomen were examples to other black women on the way to find success. Annie said that Poro saleswomen spread "the gospel of better personal appearance."

Afterwards a crowd of women came up to the podium to ask questions. This happened at every event. Most women wanted to know how to become part of the Poro team. The women came from all levels of society.

One of the women had worked in a furniture factory, hauling supplies from table to table. Three months earlier, she injured her leg on the job and was unable to continue factory work. Another woman worked as a maid, but now was caring for the baby daughter of her brother who had recently died. She needed to find work that she could do at home. Another woman, a principal in a local grade school, wanted a new career. Almost a dozen women signed up to work for Poro that afternoon.

Annie closed her eyes and patted the sweat from her face. She refolded her handkerchief and patted her neck, where beads of sweat soaked her collar.

Just then a voice said, "Nothing cools like a lemonade." Without opening her eyes, Annie could tell that the speaker was smiling; the words were spoken with such lightheartedness.

The man standing before her was indeed smiling. He held out a glass of frosty lemonade and introduced himself.

"Aaron Malone," he said, straightening his posture formally and smiling even bigger.

A handsome man with large eyes and a thick mustache, Aaron sat down beside Annie. He said he had enjoyed her speech. He especially liked the part in which Annie said that the Poro company was "more than a mere business enterprise." Poro, she had said, was "consecrated to the uplift of humanity – Race women in particular."

Aaron told Annie that she had picked an excellent time to start her company. Annie knew what he meant.

At that time, Missouri, like many other states, tried to keep the races separated. The lawmakers in Jefferson City, the state capital, passed segregation laws. In 1889, long before Annie arrived in Missouri, a law was passed ordering black and white children to attend different schools. Ordinances in St. Louis and other towns kept blacks from going into all-white hotels, restaurants, theaters and hospitals. Special real estate contracts denied blacks the right to live in certain areas of the state's cities.

Black people wanted better educational opportunities, living conditions and jobs. They also wanted better legal and social services. But they had very little power or money to change their situation. More than 90 percent of black people in St. Louis worked as domestic servants, laborers, farm hands and factory workers.

Since most lawmakers ignored them, black people began to organize. They formed political groups. In 1909/1910, the National Association for the Advancement of Colored People (NAACP) was formed. State chapters soon began in Missouri and other states. In addition, black people created social organizations and clubs to help African American orphans, the elderly, the disabled and other people whom the larger society was unwilling to help.

Annie also believed that her race needed to unite in order to improve their lives. She felt that education and financial independence would lead to political rights and social advancement. Annie also believed that Poro offered those opportunities.

Women were eager to attend Poro College and work for Poro. It was hard for a black person to find dignified, steady and well-paying work. At this time, black domestic servants earned only one or two dollars a week. Women working for Poro could make three to five dollars a day. Experienced sales women, who had many customers, could earn as much as $100 a week. Some women worked in their homes, setting up beauty parlors in their kitchens. Some became so successful that they opened Poro beauty salons.

Aaron was right. This was, indeed, an excellent time to start a company like Annie's.

Aaron asked if Poro employed men. Annie shook her head no. Two years earlier, in 1910, she had moved the company to a larger office. By then Poro was national.

The company needed the entire building at 3100 Pine Street. The company's brochures called for "ambitious women to enter a profitable profession" and promised economic independence as Poro agents.

Poro was created by a black woman for black women. Annie told Aaron that men's political and fraternal clubs sometimes met at the Pine Street building. "And I believe many husbands help their wives who are Poro agents," she added.

Aaron rubbed his chin thoughtfully and then he smiled broadly. "Guess if I want a job with Poro, I'll just have to marry the boss."

❧ *10* ☙

The Poro College Building, 1918

And that is what happened. Aaron and Annie married two years later on April 28, 1914. Hundreds of Poro workers and leaders in the St. Louis black community attended the wedding. Not as well-known as Annie Turnbo, Aaron Malone was a former schoolteacher and a traveling bible sales-

man. He knew a great deal about marketing and was eager to start working for Annie's company. In the years to come, Aaron would have an important role in helping Annie come up with ideas to develop and sell the Poro products. She made him the chief manager of the company.

65

When Annie and Aaron married, Poro was one of the most successful black companies in the country. Other businesses now offered cosmetics for black women, but none were more successful than Poro. Annie outran the competition with her system of franchised sales representatives.

Annie's products were so successful that people began trying to duplicate and sell her hair products. One woman even started a cosmetic business and gave her hair product the same name as Annie's Wonderful Hair Grower. Annie decided to protect her business. She registered the trade name, Poro, so copycats could not use it.

Four years after her marriage, Annie built the Poro College building. It was located in St. Louis's upper-middle class black neighborhood. The college occupied the entire city block at Pendleton and St. Ferdinand Avenues. Editors of the nation's black journals came to the opening of Poro College.

The three-story building became the first center in the country for training black cosmetologists. The modern building had classrooms, beauty salons, barbershops, experimental laboratories and company offices. It also had a manufacturing plant, laundry and seamstress shop.

One company brochure said,

There are one hundred rooms — cheerful, comfortable and scrupulously clean. Every Poro Agent has the privilege of coming to Poro College once every twelve months for the ten day Review Course. There are no charges for room and board while taking the Review Course, nor is there a tuition fee. Thus Poro Agents are encouraged to keep abreast with new, improved methods and to maintain the highest proficiency in their work.

Classes at the college included Scalp Culture, Manicuring, Pedicuring, Facial and Body Massaging, Marcelling, Hair Weaving, Fancy Hair-Dressing and many other beauty-care subjects. Besides learning about hair and skin care, Poro agents learned how to walk and sit correctly. They also learned to speak and dress properly.

Poro College had an auditorium, conference rooms, a gentlemen's smoking and recreation parlor, cafeteria, dining halls, ice cream parlor, bakery, emergency hospital, theater, hotel rooms and a roof garden.

Poro College became an important social hub for black people in the midwest. All sorts of groups held meetings at the college – religious, fraternal, civic, political and social.

The National Negro Business League had its head-quarters at Poro College. Black people, refused service at St. Louis all-white restaurants and hotels, found first-class accommodations at Poro.

Annie was working days and nights, sometimes sleeping only a few hours on a cot in her office. Her only day of rest was Sunday. Macie again warned Annie about quicksand. "You better slow down," Macie said. But the business was growing. Within a few years, Annie added an annex to the large Poro building. Annie was receiving wonderful reports from all over the country about women who found success working for Poro.

At Poro beauty shops, women came together for fun and fellowship. The shops also became neighborhood centers for sharing information and organizing.

Women who attended Poro College often organized clubs when they returned to their hometowns. Club members formed mutual aid societies to help each other in times of need. They raised money for churches and charities. Through the Poro College in St. Louis, they enjoyed insurance benefits.

Annie Turnbo Malone had found success. She had power and unprecedented wealth. She created uplifting opportunities for thousands of women. But Macie and her other friends were right to worry about Annie. There would be more success ahead – but there would also be, as Macie had warned, quicksand.

The illustration on the next page appeared in the 1945 program produced by the Poro Company for The Forty-Fifth Anniversary Celebration.

Guinea

Ancient
Ethiopia-
Egypt

Somali-
Ethiopia

Mangbe
Tou

Galla

Central

Tuareg
North

Zulu

Her Majesty
The Poro Graduate
The High Priestess of Beauty

PORO
SCHOOL OF BEAUTY CULTURE
HAIR AND TOILET PREPARATIONS

❧ *11* ❧

A Holiday Banquet

Annie loved candlelight. A cluster of three tall candles sat in the center of each table in Poro College's big dining room. The flickering little fires created a warm golden glow. A long garland of evergreens and holly ran down the center of the tables, filling the room with the sharp, clean smell of pine.

It was the 1925 Christmas Banquet. Every year Annie's company held a fancy dinner and awards program.

Ruby was in charge of the decorations. Moving between the linen covered tables, she softly sang a Christmas carol, "Deck the Halls with Boughs of Holly." At each table, Ruby placed gold and red balls among

the evergreens. The candlelight sparkled on the shiny surfaces of the balls.

Poro employees from everywhere attended the big banquet. The event was always festive, a time to celebrate the extraordinary achievements of the growing company. A year earlier, in 1924, Annie had traveled to Europe. She wanted to study hairstyles in England, France, Switzerland and Italy. There was now talk of opening Poro salons in Europe.

A long gold banner stretched above the head table in the dining room. Red letters spelled out: "CLEANLINESS, GOOD GROOMING, THRIFT AND INDUSTRY." This was the motto for Poro, and it was on all the company's brochures.

That motto perfectly described what Annie expected of everyone who worked for her company. Annie took a personal interest in the work and lives of her employees – some people claimed she took *too* great an interest. Annie knew the gossip…Annie T. Malone is bossy, too autocratic. Her critics said she demanded too much. She supervised the agents' training. She showed up unannounced in classrooms at the college. She led the daily chapel services at the college.

Annie walked to the podium at the head table. She spread two typewritten pages across the slanted surface.

Macie, standing in the back of the room, called to her, "Let's test the microphone, Annie. Read something from your speech."

Annie cleared her throat and the microphone crackled. From the first page, she read several underlined sentences, the theme of her speech, "We must continue to pledge ourselves to more than power and pride," she said. "For these are hollow without uplift. You and I and Poro must be a constructive force in the development of our race."

Macie sighed. She believed in the message, she believed in her boss, but...oh, she said to herself, how she wished Annie could just for once – today, for example – try to enjoy herself. For years Macie had urged Annie to be less serious. But lately Annie was more than just serious. She never thought or talked about anything but the business. She worked until late at night and on the weekends, except Sunday when she attended church. But even at church, Annie sometimes visited Sunday School classes, recruiting new sales agents or meeting with the preacher to talk about some charity that needed money from Poro.

Aaron had taken over part of the business operations. He liked meeting the city's business leaders. Consequently, he handled most of the vendors, the companies that sold supplies to Poro. Admittedly, Annie sometimes didn't like his growing involvement. But Macie was right. With the business growing so large, Annie simply couldn't do everything.

Poro was enormously successful, and Annie was a wealthy woman. By the 1920s, she was a multi-millionaire, one of the two richest women in St. Louis. The other woman was a white heiress. In 1925, Annie paid $40,000 in income tax, reported to be the most paid by one person in Missouri. She owned one of the first Rolls-Royce automobiles in St. Louis.

The Rolls Royce, manufactured in Great Britain, was one of the most expensive automobiles in the world. The model shown here is the Silver Ghost from the 1920s.

Macie looked across the room at her boss. Annie's head was barely visible above the podium. Macie called out for her to stand on the wooden box. "No one will see you if you don't. They'll think the podium's talking." For the first time, Annie smiled, and then she told Macie that she couldn't spend any more time in the dining room. She needed to get back to her office. Never a moment's rest, Macie thought.

❧ 12 ❧

Sharing the Wealth

Annie worked at her desk until the first holiday banquet guest arrived that night. She and Aaron stood by the dining room door greeting each person. Agents from as far away as New York and California arrived. Guests also included editors from black newspapers and dignitaries from the nation's black universities. Aaron, who had invited black leaders from Missouri's Republican Party and the NAACP, led them to a reserved table.

By the time dinner ended, everyone was eager to hear Annie speak. Presentation of the awards was the highlight of the evening. Several people preceded Annie. Aaron reported on the year's financial gains. Profits had almost doubled. He announced the opening of several new franchises in Los Angeles, New York City, Cleveland and Birmingham, Alabama.

Finally Annie stepped to the microphone. She looked up at the motto spelled out on the gold banner above the head table. Annie told the audience that most women who went through the Poro training lived up to the motto. She held up a piece of paper containing a long list of people who worked for the company.

"These women have shown their industry – and loyalty – to the Poro family," she said. As Annie called their names, the women formed a line across the room. Rudy handed each woman a small jeweler's box. It contained a diamond ring.

Every year at the banquet, Annie handed out diamond rings to employees who had worked at the company for five years. Annie rewarded other employees who met the company's strict standards. She gave them lavish gifts. Annie encouraged her employees to invest in real estate or help their parents to do so. At the banquet she gave gold and cash awards to employees who invested. She also rewarded agents with low-cost mortgages. Annie even awarded prizes for punctuality and attendance.

By the mid-1920s Poro employed approximately 75,000 sales agents in North and South America, Africa, the Caribbean and Philippines. In St. Louis,

175 people worked full time in the Poro College building.

Annie told the guests at the holiday banquet that Poro agents weren't just good saleswomen, they were good citizens, too. She stressed that "every Poro Agent should be an active force for good."

Annie practiced what she preached. As a deeply religious person, Annie believed she should share her wealth. Her generosity extended far beyond her

At the turn of the century, a group of St. Louis black women became concerned about the treatment of black orphans in the city. They talked to Annie. Black orphanages around the country received $5,000 or more annually from her. In 1919, Annie accepted the position as president of the St. Louis orphanage, which the concerned black women had founded. The next year Annie bought land for a new orphanage building. Annie remained president until 1943. In 1946, the home was named for Annie. The St. Louis Colored Orphans Home still operates and is now called the Annie Malone Children and Family Service Center. It is the oldest facility in St. Louis dedicated to caring for disadvantaged young people.

employees. Annie was the nation's first major black philanthropist. By the time Poro College opened in 1918, one of the nation's black newspapers noted that Annie gave more to charity than "any one hundred colored Americans in the United States."

Annie knew that most of the people in the audience also believed in helping people in need. They believed in uplifting the race. Annie urged her audience to use their profits and earnings to advance their beliefs. Who else would help black people, Annie asked, except black people who had the power to do so?

⛧ 13 ⛧

Weathering Two Storms, 1927

The sky turned dark blue. Low-hanging clouds tumbled overhead, like a boiling pot of gumbo.

That should have been a warning.

But it wasn't. Most of the workers at Poro College, seeing the afternoon sky turn almost as dark as twilight, ran up to the roof-top garden to watch the strange weather. The threatening clouds looked as if they might suddenly release a torrent of rain. But no rain came – just a stronger and stronger wind. The plants on the roof lashed about in the gales.

It was September 29, 1927. Earlier that year, terrible floods destroyed much of the Mississippi River Valley. Several hundred people drowned and 600,000 were left homeless. Twice during the summer workmen pumped flood water from Poro's laundry room. Much of Annie's charity work

turned to helping flood victims.

After a while the sky became lighter – an odd, greenish color. The wind stopped, too. The roof plants were perfectly still. Annie would never forget it – the whole world seemed motionless, as if holding its breath.

One of Poro's switchboard operators was the first to see it. She stood at the south end of the roof and pointed to a black cloud spinning toward the city. Annie watched the tall column, twisting like a snake. She called to everyone to leave the roof and run to the basement. Some people wanted to stay and see the tornado, a spinning cloud that was both frightening and fascinating to watch. Annie insisted that they go below. Even if the funnel didn't hit the Poro building, it could fling debris all around its path.

The tornado did miss Poro College, but it tore through other populated parts of St. Louis. Although the storm lasted only five minutes, it killed 87 people and injured 1,500 more. More than 1,000 homes were destroyed and property damage was $50 million.

That evening the Red Cross contacted Annie. The emergency-aid organization asked Annie if the Poro building could be used as a relief center. Actually, Annie and her staff had already started helping storm victims. They cleared furniture from the biggest rooms and set up cots and sleeping pads. The college's little hospital was opened to the public. The kitchen served food around the clock to anyone who needed a meal.

For the next few days, Poro College was an official relief site. Hundreds of tornado survivors received shelter, clothes, food and medical care.

———————

Annie spent as much time helping as she could. After all, she felt grateful that Poro and its employees were spared. But Annie wasn't entirely spared from sorrow.

Earlier in 1927, Aaron Malone filed for divorce. Aaron wanted half the business because he said he was responsible for Poro's success. The divorce proceeding was bitter and very public. It made news around the country. Even people not connected to the couple had strong feelings. For several years, Aaron had befriended national black leaders and had become well-known among some important Missouri politicians. And some people continued to believe that men were heads of their households and should have control over their wives.

On the other hand, Annie had her own supporters, including black churchmen, Poro workers, and many famous leaders, including Mary McLeod Bethune, the president of the National Association of Colored Women. Black-owned newspapers and magazines also supported Annie. One newspaper editorial said that Poro College had prospered "without the guiding hand of a man." In an article about the famous divorce, the *St. Louis Post Dispatch* later reported, "A mass meeting was held in her behalf, with prominent Negroes attending from as far away as California and Florida."

When Annie and Aaron could not reach an agreement, the court took control of Poro College. A white man was put in charge of the all-black company. A great outcry erupted in the black community. One newspaper wrote, "Madam Malone's fight becomes the Race's fight."

Annie quickly moved to find a settlement. She feared that the company, which she formed more than 30 years earlier, would be destroyed. On May 9, 1927, Aaron agreed to accept $200,000 and allow Annie to have sole ownership of Poro. Soon afterwards, a divorce was granted.

Even months later, when the tornado hit, Annie was still numb from the battles of the divorce. She knew that she was as much at fault as her husband for the failure of their marriage. One day, Macie came into Annie's office carrying a dictionary. "I've found the word I've been looking for to describe you. You are not only too serious," she said, and pointed to a word in the book, "You're also too `autocratic'."

Macie was right. Annie knew she was too bossy, too set in her ways about how things should run in the company. But knowing that didn't change anything. Annie's life, right or wrong, was Poro College. It always would be.

Annie had won. She'd retained ownership. And yet, although she won back her company, Annie was slow to recover from the divorce. Why was that? Even before the divorce, she and Aaron had quarreled. It wasn't as if she was sorry to end the marriage. So why was she slow to get back to her old self?

Annie could take Macie's criticism because she knew that Macie was her true friend. But so many people, who Annie thought were friends, had deserted her during the divorce. They had actively supported Aaron's attempt to take the business away from Annie. Annie believed that was why she still felt so hurt – as if she'd been terribly injured in a train wreck – or in a tornado.

Annie often visited the tornado victims who stayed temporarily at the college. One day, she sat beside a woman with a bandaged head and an arm in a sling. The storm had wiped out most of the woman's neighborhood, killing many of the resi-

After the Civil War, many leaders in Washington D.C. worked to integrate former slaves into the mainstream society. Their efforts led to the Civil Rights Act of 1875. This law gave black people the right to have access to public places such as restaurants and theaters. Eight years later, the U.S. Supreme Court declared the 1875 law unconstitutional. The court's action created a series of new segregation laws. Segregated restaurants, theaters and other places became legal again. Even schools were segregated. Annie and other black leaders believed that African Americans could overcome these injustices by helping each other. Consequently, she decided to turn her business into a school for the betterment of black women. The women in this photograph were among the thousands who were graduated from Poro College. The photograph appeared in the 1922 Poro Hair and Beauty Culture Handbook.

P O R O   C O L L E G E

A Poro Graduating Class

PORO Agencies are now conducted by enthusiastic Agents in every state in the United States, and in Africa, Cuba, the Bahamas, Central America, Nova Scotia, and Canada. The opportunity of the PORO Agent to render genuine service is boundless.

PORO profits bring economic independence.

dents. The woman looked as if she'd been crying. Annie said she was sorry to learn that the tornado destroyed the woman's house. The woman shook her head. She said she could rebuild a house. Her arm and head would mend. And then the woman added tearfully, "But I can't get back my friends."

Two days later, Annie found the woman smiling. She held a letter in her hand, which she waved at Annie. The letter was from the woman's sister who lived in Denver, Colorado. The sister invited the woman to come out west and live with her. "Sometimes you just have to make a fresh start," the woman said to Annie.

A few months after the tornado, Annie traveled to Chicago. She visited her friend, Claude Barnett, a leader in the city's black community. A powerful newspaperman, Barnett was the founder of the Associated Negro Press. He was also an advertising adviser to Poro College. He told Annie that she should consider moving her company headquarters to Chicago.

When she returned to St. Louis, Annie thought a long time about Barnett's suggestion. For the next two years, after Aaron's departure, Annie reorganized the company. She gave more decision-making responsibilities to her managers. She assigned several staffers to tasks that she had always done.

In 1930, she made an announcement. The Poro company – her company – would relocate to Chicago, Illinois. When a newspaper man asked why she would leave St. Louis after almost 30 years, she said simply, "Sometimes you just have to make a fresh start."

Poro College – A Constructive Force

Poro College is more than a mere business enterprise. Fostering ideals of personal beauty and tidiness, self-respect, thrift and industry, and touching the lives of millions, the Institution is a constructive force in the development of the Race.

Thousands of women and girls, serving as Poro Agents, are working out their lives in a manner to them acceptable, agreeable and profitable. Thus does the Institution make a definite economic contribution to Negro life.

To develop and maintain the very highest degree of proficiency, the personnel at Poro College is organized into a welfare association which makes for good fellowship and promotes intellectual and spiritual growth. Every employee is a member of this organization, 'The Poro Family,' the officers of which are elected annually by the membership. There are nine committees: program, music, dramatic, literary, social, house, athletic, sick, and deputation, which embrace organization

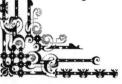

activities. Each employee is assigned to one of these committees. The committee chairmen together with the elected corps of officers constitute the 'Cabinet.' The organization pays a sick benefit.

There is an orchestra of twenty young ladies supervised by an experienced instructor and director, the instruments being provided by Mrs. Malone. A group of lady employees have, within the organization, the Porette Club, the members of which do fancy needle and other art work for charitable purposes. Tennis courts are maintained for employees.

On Christmas Eve, Mrs. Malone presents beautiful diamond rings to those whose fifth anniversary of service with the Institution has transpired during the year; to encourage thrift, she makes cash awards to those who have purchased homes or whose bank accounts show substantial savings. Trips are given for meritorious service.

Generously sharing with the public its many facilities, Poro College – vitalizing and humanizing – a center of community activity, waves aloft the standard of honest endeavor for the public good.

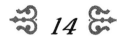

14

New Headquarters for Poro, Chicago, 1930

In 1930, Annie rented a large bus and hired a driver. She and many of her employees climbed aboard and headed to Chicago. For the next two days, while traveling, they chatted with each other and sang songs, but mostly they worked. They made final preparations to open the new world headquarters for Poro College. One press announcement said that Poro was coming "into the very heart of Negro life – Chicago's South Side."

The new Poro College, like the one in St. Louis, was a showplace. The building stood on South Parkway (now called Martin Luther King Drive), between 44th and 45th Streets. It took up an entire city block, called the Poro Block. Unlike the St. Louis college, the new Poro building looked like a giant home. A company brochure called it a mansion, "with its spacious lawns and gardens, its graceful homelike atmosphere." With Chicago as headquarters, the Poro company had branches in all the states of the union. In every major city and in hundreds of small towns, Poro agents operated Poro beauty shops and sold Poro products.

Two years after arriving in Chicago, Annie received honorary Master of Arts degrees from several schools, including Howard and Wilberforce Universities and Western and Kittrell Colleges.

Throughout her life, Annie donated many thousands of dollars to several black colleges. She gave Howard University's medical school more than $30,000 in grants. At that time, it was the largest gift ever given by a black American to a black college. Annie also supported two full-time students in every black land-grant college in the U.S.

When Annie moved to St. Louis just before the World's Fair in 1903, she dreamed of expanding her small hair-care business to black women everywhere. That dream came true – beyond anything Annie could have imagined. Thirty years later, Annie attended another world's fair: the 1933-34 World's Century of Progress Exposition in Chicago. Several national black groups and organizations attended the fair and used Poro College as their headquarters.

Six years later, Annie attended the 75th Year of Progress in Negro Achievement. It was a national conference celebrating 75 years of freedom since the end of the Civil War. Poro College exhibited at the conference. The company showed the contributions of the beauty-care industry.

In 1944, the National Beauty Culturists League invited Annie as an honored guest to its convention in Philadelphia, Pennsylvania. At the league's banquet, Annie was recognized as the black race's pioneer beauty culturist. That night her life was depicted in a musical pageant called "44 Years of Beauty Culture."

Even Annie was sometimes amazed by how much had been accomplished in 44 years. By now Poro was one of the largest employers of black people in the country. Thousands of families found financial support through their connection with Annie's company. Many households enjoyed a level of luxury they could never have achieved without their long association with Poro.

When the president of the league spoke Annie's name, the large convention hall erupted with enthusiastic applause. Everyone was on his or her feet in a standing ovation.

Annie stood in stunned silence. There were few things that Annie regretted in her life. Through the years, Annie's company had known troubles. Since her divorce, Annie had been plagued by lawsuits. A former employee sued her, claiming credit for some

Annie created Poro College to help black women. She also intended to uplift the entire black community. The college offered theater, music, art, athletics, lectures and religious services. Marian Anderson, Roland Hayes, Ethel Waters and many others performed on stage at Poro College.

of the Poro products. Another suit came from a St. Louis newspaper. These legal battles took a heavy toll on Annie's finances. She finally settled the lawsuits in 1937 by selling the St. Louis Poro College building.

But Annie wouldn't let the battles keep her from her central goal – the work of Poro. Too many people relied on Poro for a living. Too many people's hopes centered on Poro.

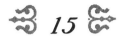

15

The Beauty of Service,
Chicago, August 25, 1950

Annie watched the little girl as she sat in her mother's lap. Annie recognized the young mother. She and *her* mother – the little girl's grandmother – ran one of the Poro salons in Philadelphia. They had taken over the business from the little girl's great-grandmother. That was three generations of women supported by Poro.

Once again the little girl's fingers moved through her mother's hair, twisting and turning it into smooth, black ropes. Would the little girl become the fourth generation to find meaningful employment through Poro?

Annie closed her eyes. She better be careful, she thought, and laughed to herself, or someone would think she'd fallen asleep, snoring away at her own anniversary party: the 50th Anniversary of Poro. Earlier Annie heard someone whisper, "That's her, isn't it? That's Mrs. Malone? Eighty years old – can you believe it?" Another voice chided, "You should look so good at 80."

Annie listened to all the speakers who praised her life's achievements. They acclaimed her success and generosity. They described the keys to Annie's success.

Once again someone at the microphone was praising Annie. The audience applauded. It was time for Annie to speak.

Key to success? As she walked to the podium, Annie thought about those words, their meaning. It wasn't about success, she decided finally. Her work – the driving force in her career – was about ser-

Annie T. Malone

vice. Annie had never asked black women to be something they were not. She didn't believe in hair straightening or skin bleaching. Annie always knew that the desire for beauty was more than vanity. Her company did more than sell cosmetics. It offered a way out of poverty and despair. It offered a way of…well, living.

After thanking everyone who had come to celebrate Poro's anniversary, Annie began to talk about the half-century history of the company.

At the end of her speech, Annie said that Poro went beyond physical beauty. Training beauty agents and sales women, Annie said, "does not confine itself to the handling of hairdressers' tools, but embraces all that the word 'beauty' implies – beauty of thought, of spirit; the beauty of cleanliness, of grace, of dignity, of Godliness: the beauty of service and above all, the beauty of living. What greater contribution could be made to an essentially beauty-loving race of people."

Postscript

Annie died of a stroke on May 12, 1957, in a Chicago hospital. At that time, Poro Schools and branch offices were in 32 cities.

This illustration appeared in the 1945 program produced by the Poro Company for The Forty-Fifth Anniversary Celebration.

J.L. Wilkerson, a native of Kentucky, now lives in Kansas City, Missouri. A former teacher, Wilkerson has worked as a writer and editor for more than 25 years. She is an award-winning writer whose essays and articles have appeared in professional journals and popular magazines in the United States and Great Britain. She is the author of several regional history books for adults. Wilkerson also has written children's books, including other biographies for Acorn Books' The Great Heartlanders Series.

Information about Annie T. Malone's life and times is available through these resources:

"The Claude A. Barnett Papers" at the Chicago Historical Society, which contain correspondence, clippings, photographs, press releases, publications and typescript biographies.

Brodie, James Michael. *Created Equal. The Lives and Ideas of Black American Innovators.* Morrow, 1993.

Fox, Timothy J. and Duane R. Sneddeker. *From the Palaces to the Pike. Visions of the 1904 World's Fair.* Missouri Historical Society. St. Louis, Missouri, 1997.

Greene, Lorenzo J., Gary R. Kremer and Antonio F. Holland. *Missouri's Black Heritage.* University of Missouri Press, Columbia and London. 1993, revised edition.

Notable American Women: The Modern Period. A Biographical Dictionary. Ed. Barbara Sicherman, Carol Hurd Green, et al. Belknap Press of Harvard University Press, 1980.

Peiss, Kathy. *Hope in a Jar. The Making of America's Beauty Culture.* Metropolitan Books, Henry Holt and Company. New York, 1998.

These and other sources were used during the research of *Story of Pride, Power and Uplift: Annie T. Malone.*

PRAISE FOR
THE GREAT HEARTLANDERS SERIES

"Although the books are clearly designed with an eye toward the classroom...they are well-written and interesting enough to capture children's imaginations on their own."
Omaha World Herald, 10/12/98.

"History comes alive in a colorful biography that follows the life of writer Mari Sandoz from her childhood on the Nebraska plains to her last years in New York as a celebrated author...In addition to being a fine biography, the book's account of Sandoz's years as a struggling writer gives the book a universal theme and presents avenues for discussion apart from the historical aspect of the story."

American Library Association, *Booklist*, 2/1/99

"The inviting formats, easy-to-read texts, and black-and-white photographs and sketches will draw both reluctant readers and report writers."

American Library Association, *School Library Journal*, 3/99

A Doctor to Her People, "with its maps, drawings, and photographs — some quite charming — packs a fair amount of information into its 100 pages...[Y]oung people who may never have heard of her will be fascinated."

American Library Association, *Booklist*, 6/1/99

"Acorn Books is doing a great service for eight-to twelve-year olds by publishing their attractive ~ Great Heartlanders Series...The care that Acorn Books takes with its books is evident. They are filled with informational maps or diagrams and include black and white photographs of many of the books' subjects."

Nebraska Library Commission ~The Nebraska Center for the Book, *NCB News*, Spring, 2000.

"Curious children will appreciate this well-done book [*A Doctor to Her People*], with its interesting pictures, maps and drawings."

Lincoln Journal Star, 7/11/99

"Acorn Books has launched an outstanding biography series for young readers called `The Great Heartlanders'."

Midwest Book Review, "Children's Bookwatch," 11/98.

"This well-written biography [*From Slave To World-Class Horseman: Tom Bass*] tells the life story of an extraordinary man who was born a slave in Missouri in 1859 and later became known throughout the world as a brilliant horseman...The fast-paced narrative includes a fair amount of fictionalized dialogue. Black-and-white photographs, reproductions, and spot drawings illustrate the text. This is the story of a compassionate man whose genius with horses will be an inspiration to youngsters."

American Library Association, *School Library Journal*, April, 2000

"*Frontier Freighter: Alexander Majors* is a superb biography and introduction to one of the men who helped shape the American west and is highly recommended for young readers ages 8 - 12."

The Midwest Book Review, "Children's Bookwatch," 7/00

"Two new books [*From Slave To World-Class Horseman: Tom Bass* and *Frontier Freighter: Alexander Majors*] are outstanding in their descriptions of dynamic personalities who, by sheer determination and talent, left lasting imprints...With drama and historic detail, Wilkerson pulls youngsters into a world where one man's [Bass's] courage and achievements broke racial barriers long before better-known black athletes Jackie Robinson and Jesse Owens...Details about Majors' personality are especially intriguing."

The Kansas City Star, August 3, 2000

ACORN BOOKS
THE GREAT HEARTLANDERS SERIES
Making history an active part of children's lives.

You can find this book and other Great Heartlanders books at your local fine bookstores.

For information about school rates for books and educational materials in THE GREAT HEARTLANDERS SERIES, contact

Acorn Books
THE GREAT HEARTLANDERS SERIES
7337 Terrace
Kansas City, MO 64114-1256

Other biographies in the series include:

Scribe of the Great Plains: Mari Sandoz
Champion of Arbor Day: J. Sterling Morton
A Doctor to Her People: Dr. Susan LaFlesche Picotte
From Slave To World-Class Horseman: Tom Bass
Frontier Freighter: Alexander Majors
Fighting Statesman: Sen. George Norris
American Illustrator: Rose O'Neill
Sad-Faced Clown: Emmett Kelly

Additional educational materials in THE GREAT HEARTLANDERS SERIES are

- ♦ Activities Books   ♦ Celebration Kits
- ♦ Maps   ♦ "Factoid" Bookmarks
- ♦ Posters

To receive a free Great Heartlanders catalog and a complete list of series books, other regional books and videos, and educational materials, write or call Acorn Books.

Toll Free: 1-888-422-0320+READ (7323)
www.acornbks.com